READING POWER

High-Tech Vehicles

Nuclear Submarines

William Amato

The Rosen Publishing Group's
PowerKids Press™
New York

Published in 2002 by The Rosen Publishing Group, Inc.
29 East 21st Street, New York, NY 10010

First Edition

Book Design: Christopher Logan

Amato, William.
Nuclear submarines / William Amato.
   p. cm. — (High-tech vehicles)
Includes bibliographical references and index.
ISBN 0-8239-6011-0 (library binding)
1. Nuclear submarines—Juvenile literature. [1. Nuclear submarines. 2.
Submarines.] I. Title.
V857.5 .A43 2001
623.8'2574—dc21

                                          2001000274

Manufactured in the United States of America

Contents

Nuclear Submarines 4

Building a Submarine 6

The Crew's Work 8

Fighting 16

Keeping the World Safe 20

Glossary 22

Resources 23

Index 24

Word Count 24

Note 24

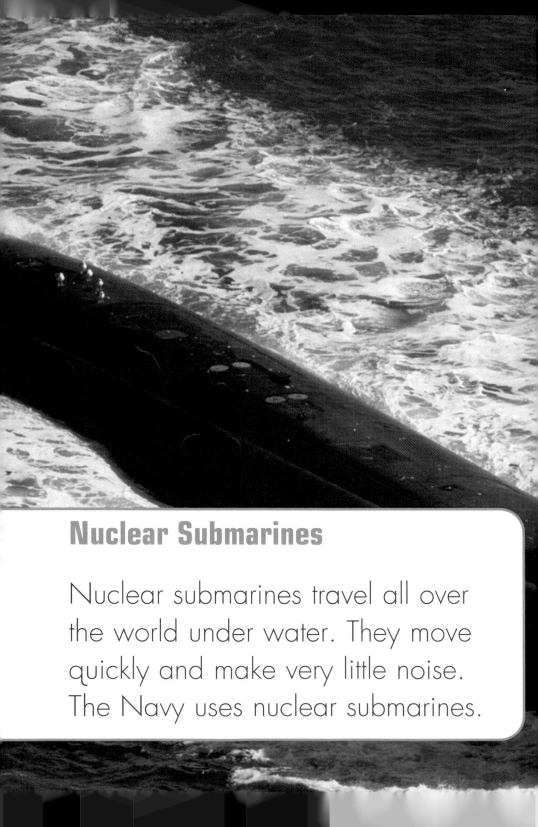

Nuclear Submarines

Nuclear submarines travel all over the world under water. They move quickly and make very little noise. The Navy uses nuclear submarines.

The word *submarine* means "below the water."

Building a Submarine

A nuclear submarine is built on land. It is built in a dry dock.

The Crew's Work

The crew uses computers to move the submarine in the water. A submarine can move forward, backward, or even up and down.

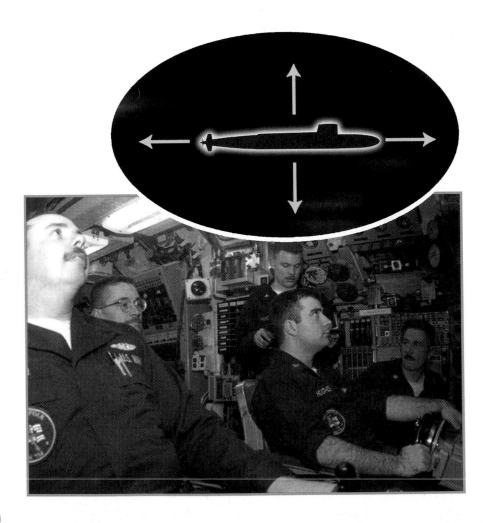

Submarines use sonar to listen for other submarines and ships. Sonar tells the crew how far away a ship is from the submarine.

Sometimes submarines use periscopes to see above the water. A sailor can use the periscope to see ships on the water.

There are more than 125 people who work on a submarine. Each person has a job to do.

The submarine is run from the control room. Here the captain gets all the information he needs to run the submarine.

The captain stands at the periscope.

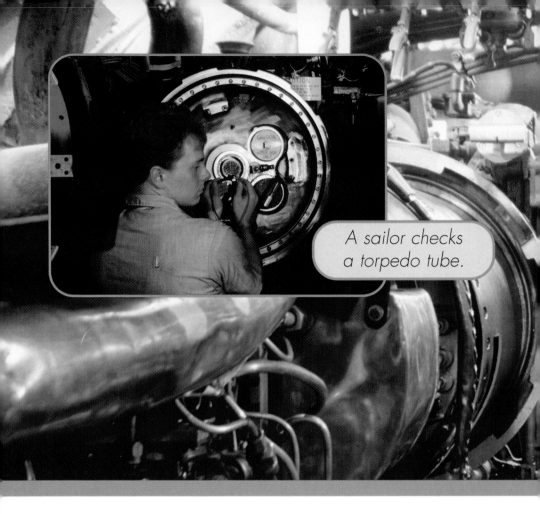

A sailor checks a torpedo tube.

Fighting

Submarines use torpedoes to fight
enemy submarines and ships.
Torpedoes look like big fish.

Torpedoes can travel as far
as five miles.

The crew puts torpedoes in special
tubes. Torpedoes are fired from the
front of the submarine.

Submarines also have missiles. Missiles can be shot from under the water into the air.

Missiles are shot
out of missile tubes.

Keeping the World Safe

Submarines are the undersea wonders of our high-tech world. They are used to keep the world safe.

Different Types of Nuclear Submarines	
Type	Length
Ohio	560 ft.
Benjamin Franklin	425 ft.
Virginia	377 ft.
Los Angeles	360 ft.
Sea Wolf	353 ft.

Glossary

crew (**kroo**) a group of people who work together

nuclear (**noo**-klee-uhr) a very powerful kind of energy

periscope (**pehr**-uh-skohp) a machine on a submarine that lets a sailor see above water

sonar (**soh**-nar) a machine on a submarine that uses sound waves to find ships in the water

Resources

Books

Submarines
by Tony Gibbons
The Lerner Publishing Group (1987)

Boats, Ships, Submarines, and Other Floating Machines
by Ian S. Graham
Larousse Kingfisher Chambers (1993)

Web Site

Submarines
http://www.pbs.org/wgbh/nova/subsecrets/

Index

C
captain, 14–15
computers, 8
crew, 8–9, 17

D
dry dock, 6

M
missiles, 18–19

N
Navy, 4

P
periscope, 10, 15

S
sailor, 10, 16
ships, 9–10, 16
sonar, 9

T
torpedoes, 16–17
tube, 16–17, 19

Word Count: 218

Note to Librarians, Teachers, and Parents

If reading is a challenge, Reading Power is a solution! Reading Power is perfect for readers who want high-interest subject matter at an accessible reading level. These fact-filled, photo-illustrated books are designed for readers who want straightforward vocabulary, engaging topics, and a manageable reading experience. With clear picture/text correspondence, leveled Reading Power books put the reader in charge. Now readers have the power to get the information they want and the skills they need in a user-friendly format.